A Lover's Truce

Kellen M. Parham

Kellen M. Parham

ISBN: 978-0-578-38663-8

Dedicated To [YOU]

This is about you and only you
No matter how hard I try
I can no longer lie
To myself
I've come to terms
With these thoughts

And they all revolve around you
Constantly spiraling
Out of control
Longing for a truce

Kellen M. Parham

Table of Contents

Kellen M. Parham

Attracted To [YOU]

Dear Kellen,

We stuck by you through all of your hype and dreams
Can't say we don't appreciate all of this
But we must admit
You are too much
And we were afraid
You wouldn't be able to handle it

We all love you
We all want
Want
The best
For you
But we didn't
Choose
To be
Your muse

Sincerely,

Your Muses (probably)

Planetary Wonders

Your eyes are two of the most beautiful planets I've ever seen!

I wish I could wrap myself within their orbit
Getting closer, gradually, gravity, grabbing me
Your aura, I absorb it

Happily, your smile brightening my space
I see our creator's ambition
Just from a glance at your face

Your perfection projecting from a billion miles away
Even if that's two decades, I'm willing to wait

The fate of our paths crossing again
On time, it all depends
Till then, I cruise to colorful hues of blues
Lay back and watch our worlds spin

Your eyes are two of the most beautiful planets I've ever seen
And it's towards your skies that I dream

In Your Orbit

Every time I rhyme
Bending
Blending space
And time
A microcosm
Of galactic energy
Overwhelms
My mind

Vivid imagery
Pink moons
Purple stars
Wrapped in blackness
Nestled
Resting
Exquisitely

Brash
Radiant
Electricity
Dazzles
Every inch of me
Overflowing
Immensely
In your orbit

Kellen M. Parham

Waiting To Wither

Tried my best to feel something today
And there was nothing
Not even an inkling
Or a sliver

If I'm blinking
I can't tell
Maybe I'm dead
Frozen
Numbed
Waiting to wither
Like a sea of wildflowers in the winter

What more can I do
To bring back the warm
Beautiful colors
I used to bloom

Flames of amber
And colorful hues of blue

Standing ready to be consumed
I realized
This is what
It must mean
To be alive
And these are just feelings of me
Sincerely, missing you

If this, in fact, is true
And my sole purpose
Is blossoming because of you

A Lover's Truce

May I never wither
May I never fade
May I blossom once again
In your presence
In your shade

Kellen M. Parham

Fuck The Metaverse, I Want You Here

Let's be honest
Well can I be?
Honestly
I'm so tired of writing
About you

Why are you constantly
On my mind
When you've never been
What the hell changed
I've never cared before

Why are you here
Where did you go
Why we not more
Like I envisioned
Though this wasn't
My intentions

You got me switching
Changing positions
I had an intuition
Something gifted
I let my guard down
And I'm wanting
You home now

I need to calm down
But I'm lost
In the sauce
Like Gucci Mane warned
How did this form
Where you come from

A Lover's Truce

You set me up
Nah, for what
I doubt it
I'm nothing special
Or am I

A Jedi
Knight
In the night
Avoiding the hype
'Cause all I dream is peace
And sleep

Don't get much of that
How can we make love from scratch
Where the recipe at
I need that

Had an idea
On how it would feel, love
But when it got here
It felt weird
'Cause it hurt
It pierced
Deep

Who's the creep
Me, nah, not you
You were cool
We'd drink
Eat
Act a fool
Hug it out
I'd carry you
Up the stairs
Til our worldly
Affairs
Cared more
Than mutual

You're what I'm trying to get into
And not virtual
Fuck the Metaverse
I want you here

Be Safe Coming Home

You're my favorite fragrance
You left your scent on my pillowcase
I pressed it firmly onto my face
Imagining your warm embrace

Waiting for you to come home
But I'm so impatient
I cry out to time
To make haste

There's a special place in my mind
Where only you reside
You bring feelings to light
Which I cannot hide

You, beautiful you
Guardian of my eyes
Protector of my thoughts
You have a heart sweeter
Than candies caramelized

If every day shall feel this way
I can't say I'll ever complain
Just don't forget to pick up your phone
When you're on the way home
And drive slow in the rain

Chocolate Daisy

I see your smile within the sunset
Your eyes dance as they glow
Your heart lies just beyond the horizon
With caution I drive slow

Intrigued by your beauty
And the wonders which it holds
You bring me warmth
As I travel down your roads

All I Ask

Be my woman baby
Nah, that line too easy
Plus I stole it
From one of my favorite songs

How about this?
You know
I've been thinking about you
Nah, you're right
That line too cheesy, too
Plus that's nothing new

What more can I say?
Hmmm, give me a second to think
Maybe there's nothing more to be said
But more so something to do

Yes, you're right, again
Something to do
More like telling the truth

Though I'd be lying
If I said I haven't been trying
But I fear I'm folding
Under the pressure

Each second
We're further apart
More separate
Hard to measure
And I'm here
Re-lying
On my same
Ol' guilty pleasures

I'm packing up my belongings
'Cause it's you I'm longing
To see
So I'm on my way
Wait for me
Patiently, as can be
That's all I ask

Let's Fly

Let's fly like birds fly
Together
No matter the weather
Let's be fly like art on a feather
Synchronized DNA
Made to make each other better

Soaring above cloudy skies
Nothing but a sea of blue when I see you
True to your heart where I reside
Warmed by your autumn eyes
Together we rise over the horizon's hue

Firefly

Trying to recapture
The night you came into my life
In the old jar
Of my heart

The light you see within me
Is just you fluttering
Lovingly

Honey, Be, Gentle

Addicted to that sense of nervousness
When you're around my heartbeat flutters
Like wings of a honey bee
Plus, you're sweet
Wanting to taste the nectar
Of your honey tree
Fully wrap myself around your limbs
Becoming one with your leaves
Wiping the pollen off of your lips
Using my kisses to fertilize your seeds

You make my heartbeat
Flutter like wings of a honey bee

Honey
Be gentle
For my heart is as fragile
As the queen bee it houses
And if you haven't noticed
You are that queen
And my face is attached to every working bee
Providing for you
I am your drone
With a vow to put my stinger
Into anyone or anything
Dying
Protecting your throne
My honor
Knowing you will live on

One day I will die for you
The thought
Makes me nervous
Of which I'm addicted

When you're around my wings flutter
Like the heartbeat of a nervous human

That sweet smell of your perfume
Is the source of my attraction
If I had hands
I would pluck every rose
From God's secret garden
That shall bloom this spring
Wishing you could understand
The love songs that I sing
But they're drowned by the sounds
Of my buzzing wings

You make my wings flutter
Like the heartbeat of a nervous human

Addicted to that sense of nervousness
Maybe it's God's will
That I'm deserving this
Or maybe someday we will
Be and flutter away together
Like wings of a honey bee

Honey, be, gentle

NDA

How am I to move on
When I'm stagnant in your memory
Bounded
By a non-disclosure agreement

I Want To Love You

You ignore me too much
But you're well intentioned
And I have no choice but to respect it

I think I want to love you
However, I must check it
I'm the married one

Who Is It?

Take me off your pedestal
I'm still a man
Lying and complaining –
The same

Driving my lover insane
Just ask her
If you don't believe me
I'm okay with taking the blame

Though I wish
I'd never succumbed to this
Not living up to all
That's picturesque

God bless the liars
The pacifiers, deniers
I'm tired of traveling down
Your troubled roads
Bestowed by troubled trolls

Hard life to hold, heavy the toll
Sitting in dread
Waiting for it all to unfold

Damn, that lie was bold
You don't even have remorse
It's always been your choice
And it shows

Why are you laughing?
Tell me the joke
Who you wanna hold?
'Cause it sholl ain't me
Who is it then?
"KP"

She, Nah

Not the baby's papi
But I'm happy
To see her face
She's so beautiful
Like her mother

I want to holler at her
Make her a little brother
I'm talking loving
Her mother

Get real, creeps
She, nah, fine as fucks
Beyond all outdoors
Want to say I want more
But I have to be real

No matter how good
You make me
Feel
Nothing I can do with you

Without you being a part of a lie
We can try
But I don't know
How long that will fly

By estimation
This situation
Won't be hidden
Long

'Cause I can't hold water
Like them old folks
Used to say

She, nah

More Than Infatuated In [YOU]

The Pleasure

Dear My Lady

(Circa 2002 at age 18.
My very first poem that I was proud of.)

If poetry was a woman you would be that art.
If love was in her body you would be her heart.
Dialects and intellects, would be thy smarts.
Only through pure romance you would conceive thy thoughts.

I can barely tell us apart, our minds
And bodies so deeply entwined.
And what we share is so divine that I must take this time,
To thank God the Almighty for making you mine.
And hopefully, we could be together until the end of time.
But baby, I love you and thank you for being my spine.

Lovin' You Forever,

Kellen

My Phenomenal Woman

(Inspired by Maya Angelou's Poem: Phenomenal Woman)

She sways with a grace which palm trees lust
Her beauty is of a harmonious place
Residing amongst tranquility and trust
Her mystical abilities
Even makes the most prophetic blush
Her actions speaks volumes
Even when her voice astounds an angelic hush
She is my phenomenal woman
Whose aspiration brightens my twilight's dusk
Thus, she is my woman
Phenomenal is she

She carries a certain dignity
That wallows through iniquity's demise
Her heart is the key to Heaven's pearly gates
The universe's tides, glides and confides in her eyes
Shooting stars, from Venus and Mars
Cataclysmically collides as she cries
Exhibiting a radiant illustrious parade of fireworks
Upon my Earthly skies
She is my phenomenal woman
Whose inspiration propels
My ambition when ambiguity arise
Thus, she is my woman
Phenomenal is she

She is every romantic fantasy
Every intrinsic daydream
And every enlightened prayer
The epitome of a lover's layer
She is where I'm ordained to be
When aimlessly lost in the utopia
Thoughts of falsity's nowhere
She is my unfailing everything
She is my phenomenal woman
Whose unyielding dreams
Are never surpassed by my unrelenting affairs
Thus, she is my woman
Phenomenal is she
Phenomenally

The Essence of Beauty

The essence of beauty, is a soul's possession, truly
Truly, an indescribable obsession
Which can only be self-derived
Inscribed within one's heart

It sits apart and resides
Enchantingly, amongst the internal laws of love
Compelling dreamers to reach new heights above
Beyond this realm of condemnation

The gratifications from this beauty, is poetic
Magnetic, mathematically inclined
Defined through its irresistibility and dynamics
Handed down through time's mechanics

Its blueprints were Heaven sent
With a midst of modern day relevance
So unique, indeed
So unique, indeed
That all of Man was created equal in its essence

All with beauty, a soul's possession
All with beauty, an indescribable obsession
All with beauty, that can only be self-derived

Inwardly, looking for that beauty
And not amongst the dreary skies
Is the key to not only finding true beauty
But true love

For true love of the self is the wealth
And the inheritance of this possession
Continue to define your own beauty
Because yours truly
You, your soul is composed of this essence
Thus, your soul's possession
Is your outward reflection

And what a **BEAUTIFUL** reflection you be
What a **BEAUTIFUL** connection we see
The connection of your mind, your body
Your spirit, and your soul
You are now 100% beauty, 100% self-derived
But I'm sure you didn't have to be told
Behold, you are alive and
Consoled by the essence of beauty

Beauty Behold

They say beauty is in the eye of the beholder
But my eyes behold you, so is it true
That the appearance of my beauty
Is only a mirror image of you

Observing while reserving my reflection
I noticed a smooth tone, condoned of your perfection
Curves so perfected and features never faulted
Seeing your illustrious stature
Is reminiscence of Queen Nefertiti's bust, once sculpted

I continue to stand in the mirror
As if my feet rest bolted
Prepossessed by your alluring body
My mind persists and consists to undress you
My hands dismiss to caress you

Becoming deeply indulged into your tranquil skin
Even deeper into your soul I seek peace within
I find sanctity amongst your hugs and kisses
You were sent to me, not through wishes
But through prayer

From numerous days of searching
I knew you were somehow meandering out there
Somewhere, destined by a divinity conquest so rare
So grateful, you are now here

In here, near and dear to my heart, and into my eyes
I realize, beauty is truly, where my solution hides
Deep into my soul, it revolutionized
I've become transformed and reborn

Into a beauty proposed to living strong
And even stronger, because no longer, shall I search
For you are the beauty, that my eyes; that I behold
Be whole of my half, as I behold you at last

Transfixed to the mirror image that reflects my task
My task of finding true love and beauty
Beauty Behold, in my eyes
The Lord has given me truly
Truly the Lord has blessed me with you
And you are my beauty

Behold

Chocolate Cherry Divine

Sweet lady who has honey for eyes
May I indulge the nectar of your hives
And as you cum by no surprise
May I lust the quivering of your thighs

I want to be in you
Like blizzards in the winter
Like July in summer
Like salt crystals forming in mines

I want to savor your flavor
The sweets of your navel
Chocolate cherry divine

Your passion fruits, citrus roots
Sweet and sour, my candy flower
You are all I crave in ways that are sublime

When you are away
It is your taste
That is across my mind
And when the taste fades
May I take another sip of your fermented time

Sweet lady who has honey for eyes
My chocolate cherry divine

Sweetest thing I've ever known
Your kiss tastes like amaretto

What's Your Fantasy?

I was asked
What's my fantasy
Well mine, is a lifetime times three thousand light years
Beyond this vexed galaxy
That holds my flesh casualty

See, my fantasy carries me
On illustrious shooting stars called dreams
To a destination where open arms are waiting
And where everything called love seems

Though this destination is of a barren illuminating planet
Never take it for granted
That I am here alone
Because this is the home of Her
This is the home of She
This is the home
Where hormones roam
And where She is on top of me
And where me is on top of She
And where We
Become One under a Sycamore tree

Entwined indeed
Entwined in leaves,
Entwined in sweat, eyes, chest, thighs and knees
Entwined in, *Let me get on top to gratify your needs.*
Entwined in, *Baby, don't stop! Keep me cumming, please!*
Entwined in, the euphoria
Of me holding Her
And the inkling of her sensual tongue
The taste of Her sweet and pleasant nectar
Is the catalyst to what's soon to come

Entwined in, mind winding, body grinding, and soul climbing
Entwined in, sexual contact
Resigned from coital climax
We relax and lay back
Reflecting upon the stars
That brought us to where we are
To this lifetime times three thousand light years
Beyond this vexed galaxy

But actually
Beyond my two closed eyelids
Resides this fantasy
And my fantasy resides within You

Love's Epiphany

Hey Slim, what's the plan for today?
The angelic voice of his female best friend
Staggered into the room
Minutes behind her flowing blonde, brown, & black
Freshly dyed, shoulder length hair
Comforting her bronze & radiant
Fairly blushed, high cheek structure
Her eyes of wits were that of Venus –
Seductive, hypnotizing, & mysterious
Her bold & prevalent, red pinkish lips
Gave Slim a sense, that they taste of pleasant
Sweet pomegranate seeds

Slim's eyes sat, anchored to her dimples
Glowing as she smiled
Slim was so intrigued by her imprisoning aura
That all sound was drowned by her presence
And Slim could only focus
On the way her red pinkish lips
Danced with her luscious tongue
As if two immortal soulful couples
Danced the tango, as she spoke

Slim….Slim… She spoke louder
Now with both hands on her hips
But still without a response from Slim
For he was now mesmerized by the way her low-cut jeans
Tightly snugged her petite & curvaceous hips
She stood in a bow-legged stance
That is only known to her
Her conflicting thighs stood parted
As if her pussy was the mediator
The ambiance of her body was the epitome of top models
God truly broke her mold

It was then, at that strange interval
Of their three-year friendship
Slim lusted her attractiveness

Her sexiness, and Slim wanted to kiss her
Kiss her tenderly, as he has kissed many others
Slim was no longer sitting
For he was floating away sexually
Drifting into a deep daydream fantasy
And as he drifts
The wind begins to howl outside his window
Dazzling rain spectacles harmonize
As they are illuminated by
The thunderous applause of lightning

As Slim continued to admire
Her red pinkish lips & luscious tongue tango
He could only imagine
They were passionately dancing to his exotic melody
Slim, I want you. I need you. Dance with me.
The warmth of the tunes overwhelmed
The boundaries of his ears
Leaving hickeys on his eardrums
Footprints down his ear canal
The arousing vibrations rambunctiously echoed
As they now, passionately dance
Through his cerebral nerves
Slim began to visualize
The depiction of his full lips & luscious tongue
Butting in for the dance
Her red pinkish lips, embraced his full lips
Her luscious tongue, embraced his luscious tongue
Their competitive tango
Became a sensual fantasy within a sensual fantasy
The lips paused to admire the tongues
The tongues paused to admire the lips
Then neither paused
For both couples were entranced
Within their own fascinations

And as they seemed to dance for hours
They must have sparked
Inspiration for the rest of the body
For they began to follow

Her cool, smooth lavender perfumed hands obliged
His warm, moist skin butter hands
The provocative smell from hand connections
Became the infamous aphrodisiac
Plundering their virginal nostrils
Consummating their thoughts
Coercing their minds to celestially dance
Their invigorated minds danced
Amongst planetary sceneries
Shooting stars even paused
To admire their eloped anatomy
As their bodies sparkled
Glistening from the dazzling rain of Earth
Their bodies became one
Unidentifiable to that of any other natural occurrence
They were truly alien
Without any human words to foretell their descriptions
And Slim wouldn't have it any other way
For she had all of him, and he had all of she
Their oneness spoke volumes
In their extraterrestrial language
And with the world at their feet
They were definitely a sight to see
For they attracted the masses
From all likes of the Earthly world
They were true exhibitionist
Lover's blind to everything beyond their reach
All they knew was each other, all they felt was each other

Their extremities continued to dance
As the dazzling rain spectacles harmonized
As the thunderous lightning applauded
And as the humans observed
Within their primitive curiosity
Slim was in complete ecstasy

Complete harmony, charting uncharted waters
Establishing new depths within his heart
Slim felt a moment of clarity
And Slim's epiphany brought him back to reality

The harmonizing spectacles of dazzling rain
And thunderous lightning applause
Became extravagant blue, sunny, clear skies,
The humans from all likes of the world
Subsided within their homes
And Slim was all alone; not holding she
But unsettling his focus on her red pinkish lips
Recognizing her body as a whole
Recognizing his best friend
He then felt a construed sense
Of guilt, anguish, and rejection
Slim hated himself, hated his decisions
Regretted how he limited his dimensions

For he traveled the walks of the world
Searching for that **One**, his true love
And that **One** he's been searching
Was next to him all along, for three years
She had been his best friend
His everything, his every desire, his every hope
What seemed to be a lifetime of a daydream
Was just a mere two seconds
As Slim dreamingly looked into her eyes
Paralyzed of words to say, and confused
All he could muster, was simply,
I Don't Know...

Hold That Pose

Some point in time
My mind
Fell into your insole

You just stood
There
For Years
Posed

I love it
Along
With everything
Above

Kellen M. Parham

Is This A Safe Space

Is this a safe space
A place accepting a writer
Who fell in love with his muse

A writer who sees the margins and the lines
But chooses to write outside of the bounds
Dismissive of the rules

Damn, I'm Just Trying to Help

Feeling sorry for your enemies
I don't have many of those
But you may not be
As fortunate

Let them talk
Listen with
Sincere, empathy
But to their victims
Not to them
Watch how they get shook

Look, at their eyes
It'll tell you all
You need to know

For example
My eyes looked right
At an angle
When I lied to my wife

Sorry
This is my life
And I can only talk about what's real

This is totally not about me
I'm just a messenger
A horse
With the bad grill
That you're not supposed to look into
But, truth be real
How are you supposed to feel?

Reading my mess

Platonic Love

[Name redacted]
I think about you
Every fucking day, and
Night
Can't sleep
'Cause I just want to see you

A thousand deleted text
That I could have written you
But I didn't want to overwhelm
Or overstep
Boo

You're so fucking beautiful to me
Told you I'd write this down

Lovers

Teach me
What my eyes can't see

Reach me
In my fantasy

Kiss me
No need for privacy

Lovers love
Even
Blindingly

Treasure

Let's stop beating around the bush
You and me
Full bloomed
The fragrance is lush

You smell good to me
Can't not want you
Here with me
Sensually

I'm writing you poetry
Though I said I wouldn't
I lied as though I couldn't

Baby, I'm here
Wanting you near
At all odd
Times

Night or day
Come my way
Please

Endless

Desert sands
Dance
Swirling
As the wind blows

Who knows
When this spinning globe
Which holds us all
Shall stall
And erode

Returning us back
To our desert
Homes
With only bones
To show
And tell
Our story

Why are we in a hurry?
The morning
After glory
Will still be cooled
By dew
Of last night's
Mist

Enjoy this bliss
While time permits
You never know
We may have lucked
Into something endless

Kellen M. Parham

An Untimely Death Is My Only Fear

Sincerely in the morning
I'll miss you much
Thinking about you all day
About our last touch
I still remember how you smell
And it's been months

Watching you spread skin butter
Over your palms
Between your fingers
Onto your arms
The little that's left
These the last images
Of my last last breath

I still don't know how you feel
I dream you're soft
Cool, smooth, to the touch
Tell me enough
If this is true
Fantasizing being next to you

By Choice Or Is It

Freeing my mind
To free my heart
Who would've thought
I'd be where I am

Sunk into your dreamy eyes
And haven't been the same since
Lost every sense of time
And language
To describe these feelings I hide

Speaking from the dark
Calling out your name
But only hearing echoes
Of my own vocals
Yet, somehow, hopeful
I remain

Though I'm bound
By no ball or chain
Not having the gall or aim
To move on
Dissolves desires to refrain
From thinking of you
Again, again and again

Kellen M. Parham

Things I Want To Say To [YOU]

The Heart Strings

Must Be Nice

Envying the skin butter cream
You rub all over your hands

Its closeness to you
Feeling your warmth

Infusing with your essence

Hands Feel

Just a chance

To live
Or
Half live

To feel
Or
Half feel

Real
Or
Half real

Dreams
Awakened
To realities
Come true

Feelings
Of
You
And
How your hands
Feel

[useless]

You're the first and last thing
On my mind every day
And there's absolutely nothing
You can do with this information

So I'm writing it here
For safe keepings
Until the time
You no longer find this useless

[Name Redacted]

Wrote you a poem as a DM
But I pressed the wrong button
And it was deleted
Wish I remembered it

Trying to be honest
But to be honest
This sucks

I wrote you something
Much, much
Better

Wish this wasn't
Part of what I had to say
Clarifying, my negligence
Yeah, my day-to-day

Clumsy
Absent minded
Mind it, is not always easy
But when I see your face

I talk cash shit
'Cause they have to believe me
When I say
You're beautiful

And I believe
When you breathe
There's a chance
Out there
For you and me

Hmmm

There is absolutely nothing rational about how much I think
about you!

But as I put rhyme to pen
The tetrahedral stylings of my complex thoughts
Kindly blend, adding up perfectly

However, this is no quick maff

Calibrating for best precision
I'm a literal mathematician
Adjusting angulations of my path
In hopes to avoid asteroids of my past

You're like the light at the end of time
I'm drawn near
Like the height of peak consciousness
It's beyond clear

That you got the juice
Tell me more of what Erykah Badu said to do
Cuz that shit's working (lol)

Even though it perceives me
That you don't believe me
I'm compelled to speak on all that's certain

I'm a literal mathematician
Rationalizing thoughts
Of U-N-I together
Like we are unity's juxtaposition
And if we were to adhere to all that I've mentioned
We shall cross paths in an all new dimension

Not Again

Thought by sending you these poems
My poetry would highlight
How much you mean to me

Hoping it'll allow
Allow you to see
Just how much
I'm thinking about you

You got me
Just as concerned
As I think you'd be
Even though
I question
If you'd love me

I'm unsure
Too afraid to truly find out
So I get high
And pretend
You'd never leave my side

Intuitively
I only want to wake to your eyes
Cuddling
Pacing your thighs
Small talk
In-between
Falling back to sleep
Wanting rest
But wanting you more

A Lover's Truce

Thus wrestling
Every
Waking
Moment
To see you
As I once saw you
Moments
Before

Baby don't leave
I can't bare
To leave you again
Come closer
I've learned from the last time
That I can't do this
Hugging you tightly
Not knowing
If I'd ever see you
Again

Again
Thought by sending you these poems
My poetry would highlight
How much you mean to me

Hoping it'll allow
Allow you to see
Just how much
Thinking about you

You got me
Every second
Every day
I've been asleep before
Thought it was promising
But I'm promising
Not again

[Name Redacted] 2

Dear [Name Redacted],

So many things I want to tell you
However, I promised to not disclose them
Holding up my end of the bargain
It's funny seeing you don't care
Admirable, it is
For sure
But fair

[Name Redacted]
Thinking about your beautiful eyes
Soft thighs
What were you expecting of me
Someone admiring you
Wanting you
To want me

Hey [Name Redacted]
Please
Be nice
Enticingly
But my expectations are low

I hardly know, you
Can't necessarily be trusted
Though you're beautiful
And that makes me weak

But weep over you
That will never be true
Never happen
Sidenote –
My good friend's brother
Didn't trust you
But I told him
You're good people

So I'm watching
Your every move
Your lingo
I'm decoding –
I heard that
Say it again

[Name Redacted]
Please be patient
With this traveling mind
Be peaceful
I'm all over the place

Scattered brained
Deranged, nah, definitely not
I'm right on spot
My eyes on you
I got

But don't want them to be
Feels I have no choice
No matter how hard I've tried
To scream
Haven't heard my voice

In years
Several months
Beaucoup weeks
I'm weak
Like I got the mumps
When it comes to you

[Name Redacted]
Stop being weird to me (lol)
Come home to me
It's enough room for you
And for things to come true
Like
Your dreams

Before Life Dims

Insecure
Immature
Hoping in the end
All of these thoughts were
Worth it

Perfect
Dreaming
I do
But I'm afraid
I'm lost
Searching for you

Beyond
The overgrown path
A love I can't grasp
Hidden like a treasure
Amongst me
And the jungle's wrath

Yearning for direction
A clue
A map
So I'm not second-guessing
This infectious
Obsession

There's a lesson
Here, I'm sure of it
Be it
A curse
Or
A purse
Full of gems

A Lover's Truce

One day
I'll find you
Before my
Life dims

Let Me Sleep

It's all a dream
It's all a dream
You here with me
Is all it seems

Your body I feel
This can't be real
It's all a dream
It's all a dream

All I ever wanted
This can't be real
Is all it seems
Your heart I feel
Is all I mean

You here with me
I can't believe
These were all the things
I felt calling me

If it's all a dream
If it's all a dream
Please don't try to wake me
Watch me sleep
Don't change a thing
Is all I mean

Finally, I don't feel sad
Now that I have you back
In my arms
It's been too long
I haven't slept this good
Since you've been gone

Please don't wake me
If it's all a dream
I want this to be
All I see

You're the love of my life
Is all I mean
To have you here
Next to me
Don't call it a dream
Though that's how it seems

Just let me sleep

I Wasn't Dreaming

You know it was a joke
A euphemism
Nothing meant
To be taken
Literally

I know what I said
But what I said
Wasn't meant
To be taken
Cynically

Though
These words
Are documented
Digitally

The utility
Of my profession
Of having you
Next to me
Isn't specifically
Sexually

I just want to cuddle
Have you caressing me
'Cause your skin
Is smooth

Too much to lose
You
You
You
You

Beautiful
You
Dreams come true
Right?

Or was I too – dreaming?

Kellen M. Parham

Don't Want to Lose [YOU]

The Pressure

Thought I Was Your Muse

Didn't choose
To be your muse
Blind-sided
By your beautiful words
Yes, I want you to hold me
Use me as your verbs

Wait
This isn't about me
Doesn't sound anything like me
Who is she
Why are you talking like this
This isn't what you promised me
Kellen
Please explain
Am I not your muse?
Who are you writing about?

Go Home

You know what's funny
Nobody has called me out
Called me toxic
Maybe I'm doing something right

Believe it or not
I'm doing it
Nah, I'm not
It's hard for me too
What were you going to say

I did what
With who
Whom
Yes, it was fun

If you're willing to tell it right
Can't trust you
With my truth
We were all night
Made her feel alright
Better

She was wet
Wetter
Than she said she was ever before
So she told me
Hold me
She held me
She was warm

I thought to perform
But I chose
To be
Authentic

Please
Go
Home

When The Well Ran Dry

The further we drift
In this desert
The less inspired
We become

Staring, partially
Upon the sun's
Wondrous
Might
Questioning

What do we do
When our well runs dry
When the heat
Burns our feet
Scorches our wings
Before we can catch flight

What do we do
When our well runs dry
And the only clouds in the sky
Are the ashes of our burning feathers

A shadowy reminder
We're bound to these sands
By a formidable tether
Covered in dust
Losing us
Possibly forever

Where does the hope go
Were they, too, burned away with the dreams
Or will hope return
Reincarnated in the form of other things

What have we done
Since our well ran dry
With the little fabric of hope we had left
Together we tied
Kept our heads held high
We caught the strongest desert wind
And now together we glide

To an oasis
Where we shall
Forever
Reside

Kellen M. Parham

One Sided Love (Closed Out)

It's never a good thing
Though it feels nice
To be kissed
Late at night
Even though it was initiated by me
And knowing you only did it reluctantly

Often I question
Whether you even feel
Are we even real?
Our love – does it exist?
'Cause abruptly
You turned away, went to sleep
As though I was dismissed
And if I didn't ask
Know what, never mind
I can't even remember the last time
You even hugged me
Softly

Have you ever missed me?
Doesn't seem like it
At least not the times you've been gone
You didn't even kiss me
When you came home

You say your love language isn't touch
Then what is it
'Cause I'm going down the list
And I'm not seeing much

Funny you once told me
Your love language was silence
Be it, I may talk a lot
And you
Never

A Lover's Truce

But when you do
It's not with sincerity
Usually a joke
Or a complaint
Or a huff
You roll your eyes
You puff
You smack your teeth
What's really going on?
What's buried deep beneath?

Talk to me
What are you writing?
Nothing!

Okay, I see
Here you go again
Closing me out
Wish I could've said that
Surprisingly

Kellen M. Parham

The Gift Giver

Times like this
I wonder if I'm just incapable of loving you
Causing conflict
Is all I seem to ever do

Perhaps, this is true
But I don't actually think that's the case
10 years – not long enough
These memories can't be replaced

No longer your time I want to waste
Where do we go from here
What's holding us back
Keeping us from ripping off the Band-Aid

Is it fear
Or is it contentment
How long have you lived
With this resentment

Your persistence to make things better
Followed by my hollowed ignorance
Are the only things
That remains consistent

Thought ignorance was bliss
But a beautiful day turned dreary
I don't want to live like this
So I get lost in the music
'Cause I need the fix

It's almost Christmas
I sent off a letter
Maybe Santa
Will fix us
Hopefully
You enjoy the gift

I'm Trying

It's all for you
Every piece
Every line
Every word
That I'm minding

Thought you knew
It's all for you
This heart
This eye
This tear
I'm crying

I crawled onto
The mountain's view
To catch your glimpse
Feels, 'though I'm dying

It's all for you
The effort
The inspiration
The passion

Thought you knew
It's all for you

Can't
You
See

I'm trying

This Book Is About You

I want to do right
But I really don't
I really want to write
But I know I won't

How long
Is too long
To be thinking
About her

It's been months
Said it before
But it's been four
And I anticipate much more

Where did my world go
I was spiritual
Now I'm pitiful
Love was plentiful
Now I'm revengeful
Full of gloom
In the full moon
Hoping love bloom

I pray you'd be
Home soon
But you're not
I think a lot
About, us
What we could be

Wish you could see, it
The way I do
Joy and pleasure
Just you and me
Me and you

A Lover's Truce

Futures
So many to choose
Too many to lose
Which one
Contains you
Loving me
The way
I want you to

Can you give me a clue
I know this isn't something
That you're used to
But I'm used to
Communicating
Keeping lines open
Mind focused
On what matters

And my focus is you
And always will be
See all of these poems
Is about us
And what we could be

Love's A Beach

All I needed was a pen
Didn't need a notepad
Wrote you love notes
On anything I could grab

Thinking about those times
Reminiscing on the blues
No matter how much pain you caused
You'll never be in *The Over [YOUs]*

Baby we used to cruise
Remember your hair blowing in the wind
'Cause your car didn't have AC back then
Yet we still headed to Tybee's beach
Late, spring break to escape the heat

We held each other through wavy wakes
Gripped the sand between our toes
Sneezed as salt water and particles of sand
Tickled our noses –
While we wished life was always roses

You were smelling mighty fine
Your warm embrace in the cold waters
Were only mine
Happiest of times
Were they not

Though you almost drowned
From that one wave
It was big
You sucked in a lot water
Had you blowing snot

Sorry I couldn't help myself
But this is between you and I
Don't be shy now
Heaven knows
How we were
One of those dreamy couples
Head in the clouds

Then, true to gravity
Somewhere we came crashing down
Felt like the grips of a chain
Pulled us back to Earth

Ashamed
Not knowing our worth
We tried to love each other

Yet
Today we hurt

Kellen M. Parham

Take Your Time, Babe

Don't go bringing me down
Don't go breaking my heart, baby
Always wished I could write songs
So maybe this is a start, baby

Hold me how
You used to when it's cold inside
Oh wow, you don't know me now
Bold, so vile
Hurting behind cracked smiles

Wishing we were more than
Images of my dream
Reminiscing on our good days
Scrolling through pictures
Of you on my screen

Tell me
Where did your love go
Where is it vacationing
Probably nowhere
You and I, together, seen

I bet the weather's nice
Beautiful sands
Covered by white clouds
I bet it's relaxing, peaceful
Pleasured and worthwhile
Serene

A Lover's Truce

Doing things
I'd never do
Acting unusual

Seeing your happiness is
Beautiful
You deserve it
That much is true

Take all the time you need

Kellen M. Parham

Obsessing Over
[YOU]

A Cautionary Tale
That I ignore
So well

She got me writing poetry
In the club

Absolutely

You probably think
This tweet is about you
Well, beloved, you're right
You're all I see
Ever since that night

You came into my life

Bruh

I can't stop thinking about you
No matter where I'm at
What the fuck is up with that?

How I'm supposed to move on
And go back?

All I see is your face
Silhouettes of your trace
When the light falls

When it's day time, I blink longer
Cuz I'm lost in a dream state
Thinking about you....

Fuck....

Thoughts In The Section

Is it Christmas yet?
It is...

I want what's on my left
I want what's on my right
I want them both
This ain't gone stop

Christmas, yes.

Little Spoon

Please, bring out the old me
The uncontrolled me
God's beautiful little spoon
Soft caresses
Can you hold me?

The tips of our tongues confessing
As the heat of our lungs undressing
Yes! You and I, we make beautiful art
Of synchronous duplexity

I can't fathom what's at the end of our destiny
As my heart questions in perplexity,
How shall you end up next to me?

Shots in The Dark

Shots in the dark is what got me here tonight
Your intoxicating allure
My heart's Kryptonite
If words I've been holding deep shall slip tonight
It definitely wouldn't be from the liquor
But from the look of, your caramel sweet delight

Hopefully, if not me
May my thoughts lay
Parallel on your sheets tonight

Hopefully, if not me
May it be my thoughts
You'd ask, *Can you squeeze me tight?*

Shots in the dark, yet your scene is bright
Conversations in slow motion
Are we?
We dreaming – right?

Surreal are the chills, l feel
Tingling nice
Another shot in the dark
So we can sing this twice

Precaution

Understand
Do you understand
Understand
Do you understand
Understand
Do you understand
Understand
Understand

God got a plan
Do you understand
God got a plan
Do you understand
God got a plan
Do you understand
Understand
Understand

Brake lights shining
Brake lights flashing
Brake lights shining
Brake lights flashing
Brake lights shining
Brake lights flashing
Flashing
Flashing
Flashing
Flashing

Thinking I'm over you
But here I go crashing
Thinking I'm over you
But here I go crashing
Thinking I'm over you
But here I go crashing
Crashing
Crashing
Crashing
Crashing

God got a plan
You don't understand
God got a plan
You don't understand
God got a plan
You don't understand
Understand
Understand

Life as you know it
Gone be over man
Life as you know it
Gone be over man
Life as you know it
Gone be over man
Over man
Over man

God got a plan
You need to understand
Understand
Understand

Crash

Save me
Save me from doing a bad thing
'Cause I'll do
Anything for you
Do anything for you
To have me
I'll do anything
To be where you are

Can you blame me
Blame me
There has to be
Has to be something
Some form of understanding

But in the back
The back of my mind
A voice shames me
Shames me into
Changing
Changing my outlook
On things I had knew
Thoughts of that
That I could have you
Have you while I'm speeding
Speeding
In the fast lane

But it looks as though
Looks as though
I'm going to pass you
Pass you
Driving too fast
Drinking
Thinking
Hoping
I don't
I don't...

Sounds of a crash

Kellen M. Parham

The Over [YOUs]

I'm never over you
I don't care what this chapter says
Look at me
Have I ever lied?

Trust me, it's all okay
We just need some
Time, together
Without the outside pressure

I'm never over you
Wouldn't lie like that
It's true

Next Chapter

I know I said some things
Done some things
But I don't regret it
The times we shared
I won't forget it

Your mind
Your energy
All magnetic
Kinetically
I'm still floating
In the direction
We were both headed

So I hope you meet me there
My true intentions
Did I mention
My plans are to keep you near
Close in my heart
With the love we share

Is that not fair, enough
Do you even care, enough
To engage the thoughts
Pouring from my heart
Or is it my destiny
That this isn't what you want

I pray it's not the latter
But if it is
I won't press the matter
Just know we were nice while we lasted
A fantastic chapter

Kellen M. Parham

Public Display of Affection

It can't just be me
Moving along
Shouldn't be me
Moving alone

Not when I call you my partner
I shouldn't be
Just hanging on

Why can't you hold my hand
Sing me songs
Am I doing something wrong
Is our house not a home

If our love is a marathon
Then why are you sprinting
What's so happy about us ending
What are you really thinking

Why are you smiling
Do you not feel the strain
Of our divide
And when I try to talk
Where do you run, hide

Late night
I close my eyes
To pray
That someday
You'd realize

A Lover's Truce

One day
I'll be gone
In another direction
No longer longing
For you
To display
Your affection

Just Say It

If this is no longer a ride
That you decide
You want to stay on
Just say it

It's okay
I can handle it

It's Over, Obviously

How many
Which number is this
I lost count
And I'm sure you're not reading this

You didn't even buy this book
Which makes it better
'Cause now I can feel free to say more
More than
Anything I'd say before

Though
I'll keep redacting your name
Out of respect
And for the fact
That you don't deserve
This power

You don't need to know
How you've influenced me
Not when
You don't give a shit
About you and me
I'm just another pawn
To you
I assume

But I don't play games
Used to want you home
But now want to be left alone
Funny, you didn't notice
Much

Missing my kisses
Falling for me
You were once
A klutz
What happened to us

It's obvious
It's over

I Don't Care

Can't have you
I want you
Every second
Every minute
Every hour
Regardless if you care

I don't care
'Cause I want you
Every second
Every minute
Every hour
Just to hold you
And share
My true love

You refuse
Me
Another one is on her way
No hesitation
She'll hear my dedication

But I only want you
I only love you

Soul of The Earth

If I could touch one thing
It would be the soul of the Earth

To get a true feeling
Of what this bullshit's worth

Not Your Muse

(She sat on my lap – I typed everything she said)

Am I too much?
Do I touch you too much?
Do I talk too much?
How much is such
That'll make you want me?
Make you need me and long for me?
Maybe because I think about you more than I think about me

What am I doing this for?
This kiss wasn't good enough
As I rubbed your feet

So I took a walk in my new high heels
And basketball shorts
But whatever

I am not the inspiration for your poetry
That is not what I am here for
So stop
Stop
Stop
No
I'm serious
I really don't like this
So Kellen stop this
You are such an asshole

Moving On, Maybe

Woke up again this morning
With the thought of you
On my mind
But not as strong
As yesterday
Not as strong, this time

Maybe I'm turning a corner
Maybe I'm finally moving on
Maybe I'm over you
Or maybe I'm wrong

But today, baby, I'm promising
I'm no longer sticking around
So I'll hold you how
You've asked before
As though it's cold inside

But only for a little while
'Cause today, remember
I'm moving on
Moving along
To the warm outside
Embracing the sunshine
Putting these desires aside

The Night Sea

Soon as I think I'm finally over you
Here you come popping up
Out the ocean blue
And just as you were here
You disappear without a *Poof!*

As tragic as it might be
Drifting lost on the night sea
Knowing you are out there, somewhere
Is the only thought that ignites me

You give me the confidence, nightly
To take a deep breath, dive in
Unafraid of death, to reach the depths
Of where you might be

Despite the odds
And barrage of waves
Thunderously crashing
The fogs of haze
I'm at peace in your presence
I'm at peace in your gaze

Pricey

Doing right
With no end in sight
Of doing wrong
Everything
Reminds me of you
Every song

It pains me deeply
Knowing I'm leaving
Wanting what I can't have
But yet
Still believing

Can't say if that'll ever change
If only I could rearrange
My choices

Missing you
I'm thoughtless
More
As each second fades
To feel a love
You can't have
Feels like death
In many ways

You're the drug
I deeply indulge
Increasing the volume
Hoping the music
Drowns out
These stubborn feelings
That don't budge
Only bulge

A Lover's Truce

Before I walked
Out of your door
I made sure
To squeeze you tightly
Pain is the cost
Of freedom
Of which
I'm paying nightly

Kellen M. Parham

Filibuster In Hopes She'd Stay

Baby, you know
That I'm trying
So
I don't understand
Why we got to fight

Baby, you know
I think you're beautiful
So
I don't understand
Why you're not smiling bright

Baby, I hope that I'm right
And you see it
The way
That I do
But your actions
Lately
Has been showing
That's far from truth

How can we bridge this gap?
And bring us back
To where
We used to be?

You said, you just can't see
Any
Future
Between us
Living happily

Can't say that I agree
We're so peaceful
In our sleep
Your soft fingertips
Running deep

A Lover's Truce

Sensual kisses
On your cheek
Unconsciously
Our bodies
Creep

I'm convinced
This is not you
This is not me
It's not our actions

Maybe, I'm convinced
These are imaginary
Satisfactions

Where do we go from here?
How do we sleep?
I wake up in night terrors
Unaware of
How deep
Our traumas build despair
Casting shadows
On our sheets

Afraid of the dark
My whole life
Afraid to go to sleep
I might die before I wake
Thus
Why I pray constantly

Prayer
Didn't used to know its purpose
It's just what was told to me
The way I was raised
By a mother blessed
Abundantly

Step daddy raised a man
He's the reason

That I'm free
If I ever had to die
He taught me
How to bleed

But none of this is
The point
Talking tangentially
To get more
Time with you
Don't move
Stay

Please
Cold hands
I'd warm with ease
How was your day?

Are you hungry?
I cooked
Your favorite meal
Not 'cause you were stopping by
But 'cause I was legit in the mood

Can't stand when you catch me in a lie
No matter how hard I try
You figure it out
You know my thoughts
Before I know my own

You're leaving?
Oh, wait!
I have a little more to say
The weather was sure beautiful
And you didn't tell me about your day

A Lover's Truce

Why such the long face?
You look tired
Maybe you should rest
Before you got here
I washed the sheets
The comforter still smells fresh

No, please wait
Don't leave
Okay, okay
What I've been meaning to say
Is that
I'm sorry

So can you
Please stay

Celebration

Finding happiness
At what cost
Breaking your heart
Another expense
Written off

Lost in this daze
For days
Thoughts crowding me
Cloudy speech
Floating
High
Solemnly

I don't even think
I possess remorse
Leaving
Has always been my choice

Just wish it was easy
A mutual divorce
But I'm too timid
Weak
Scared
You've yearned for my love
But I haven't cared

You deserve better than me
Yes, you truly do
Someone as intimate and true
Someone just as sweet too

A Lover's Truce

Everything I've despised
I see, when I look into my eyes
I brush my teeth
With my eyes closed
I'm too pussy for you
You deserve more
Better

So tonight, we're celebrating
Your divorce
Cheers to your happiness
To your future
It's brighter than ever
I love you

If I Was Her

You only want me around
When she's not around
If she's not in town

Making excuses to text me,
  Hey, you like their sound?

Screenshot of your favorite song
Screenshot of your favorite poem
I listen to it
I read it
Wondering if you mean it
Knowing I don't need it

The pressure
The pleasure
The back & forth
Tugging of our heart strings

Rings mean eternity
Where's yours?
I thought flames burned eternally
Then why is it so hard to see
In the dark
With you right in front of me?

What do you want from me!?
Wantingly to ask
But not to make it weird
'Cause I do enjoy your company

You comfort me
More than I expected
But I can't tell you that
'Cause,
What are you going to do with that?

A Lover's Truce

Another useless fact
You have many of those
I know 'cause you told me so
To be honest, I'm waiting on a new one

But I do question –
Are you man enough
To accept the choices that you've made?
Can you plan enough
To build the bed that can't be unmade?

I wonder if you're wondering
If I'm wondering
That if you're wondering
Do you really care

What's your angle?
What are you trying to get?
What if I fall for you?
How involved you'd get?

Which is true:
Do you have a lot to lose
Or do you not have a clue?

You have what others wish for
So are you sure this is what you want to do?
Are you a fool?
Well, are you?
Are you?
And do you think I'm one too?

I want to
No
I want you
To want to
Want to
Do
The right thing,
KP

Don't play these games with me
You harp on how you're grown
Just go home
Stop playing with me

Memories of you laying with me
Feeling your eyes
Watching me pretend to sleep
Was eerily sweet

Did you think it made me feel beautiful?
I woke up feeling unusual
These are things I don't do
And then you told me dreams come true

One night I dreamt of you.
 We laid in bed facing each other.
 I guess dreams do come true.

Something like that
Is what you said
As we laid, facing in the bed

What do you really think of me?
Am I one or how many?
I definitely know you have one
But, who else you're laying with
I don't really know you
Like at all
Really
Do you feel silly
As I do reading my thoughts

A Lover's Truce

How are you justifying this?
How many internal battles have you fought?
To say no
I didn't sense a struggle
Though you were ready
I removed your hand
And kept the night steady

Now you're home writing more poetry about me
You made this one clear since September
It's damn near December
How much longer will this last?

If I Was Him

Wondering what you feel
When I'm in your presence
Is it that same chill
Running the length of my neck
Running down yours?

Too busy lost inside of your eyes
I didn't realize
That I don't even know
How your hands feel

Are they soft?
Are they smooth?
Are they warm?
Are they cool?

Photographic memories
Of you are blinding
I can no longer see the world around me
And now your face is more vivid
Than the moon's shining

Wanting you deeper than ever
I may never regain control
Thinking of, when is the next time
Your body I'd get to hold

The grips of your smile
Just won't let me go
It's like you're here with me
Everywhere I go
You're in the passenger seat
I'm driving slow
Singing a song to you
Wishing I belonged to you

I miss your eyes

A Lover's Truce

Flames of amber
Piercing through my soul
Missing your laughter echoing
Through my hollow door

Wish I could rewind the night
Relive it in an endless loop
Still more depths of you
I'd like to explore

Chartered ships
Leave your hips
Fingertips
Kissing your shores

Do you feel my kisses?
Or are thoughts of me that easily ignored?
When you see your reflection in my eyes
Is it everything you've wished for?
Or is it much more?

I can go on and on
But I'm not sure
How much more
You can afford

So let me leave this here
And we won't have to talk about this
Anymore

About The Author

    Kellen M. Parham was born in Atlanta, GA, but partially raised in Lil Brooklyn, New Iberia, LA. He learned to harness the gift of writing while studying Mathematics at The Georgia Southern University (#GATA). Mathematics and statistics pays his bills, but it's through poetry where he finds purpose and freedom. Getting lost into his deepest thoughts is all he ever desires. Being honest and documenting those thoughts may end up being his downfall, but it's a risk he's willing to take. Embrace every thought you have he suggests – the good, the bad, & the unacceptable. Stop fighting them. Come to a truce. This is his truce. His coming to peace. No matter the cost. He loves his family and he loves [YOU].

www.ingramcontent.com/pod-product-compliance
Lightning Source LLC
Chambersburg PA
CBHW061148040426
42445CB00013B/1611